Teaching in a Classroom of Diverse Learners

A sourcebook of examples, ideas and strategies as well as ready-to-use graphic organizers and rubrics

Written by Victoria Quigley Forbes
and Marilyn K. Smith

Illustrated by Mark Gutierrez

D1561056

Teaching & Learning Company
1204 Buchanan St., P.O. Box 10
Carthage, IL 62321-0010

This book belongs to

_____

Cover by Mark Gutierrez

Copyright © 1998, Teaching & Learning Company

ISBN No. 1-57310-111-7

Printing No. 987654321

Teaching & Learning Company
1204 Buchanan St., P.O. Box 10
Carthage, IL 62321-0010

Table of Contents

Dear Teacher or Parent,

As teachers, we have been faced with many changes in the educational world. One aspect never changes. There are always a handful of students that "just don't get it." This could include learning disabled students, slow learners, remedial students and any other at-risk students. Therefore, we developed this book to provide instant, hands-on strategies and techniques to meet the immediate needs of these students.

How many times have you asked a child to complete a task in your classroom only to have the child interpret it differently than you intended? How did you respond? Was your first reaction negative? Did you think the child was being defiant or seeking attention? If so, you are not alone.

Some children's perceptions are often different than expected. Teachers need to be aware of these students in their classrooms. Do the following examples sound familiar?

- You ask a student to put his name on top of the paper. As you walk around to monitor, you notice that his name is in the middle of the paper. When you ask him why, he replies, "It is on top." (The child thinks you meant anywhere on the side that is facing up—the top side of the paper.)

- You ask a student to write a paragraph with at least three sentences. In a very short time he announces he is done. You look at his paper and he has written three *lines*.

- You give very explicit directions with examples. You ask if there are any questions about the assignment. A student raises her hand and replies, "I don't understand." You ask, "What don't you understand?" She gives you a blank look. (The student is thinking to herself, "I asked the question. Why is she asking me a question?")

These kinds of misconstrued perceptions are what led us to change our teaching and interactions with our students in order to enable them all to succeed in a typical classroom. Please feel free to reproduce, change or adapt any of our strategies to meet the individual needs of your students.

Sincerely,

Victoria & Marilyn

Victoria Quigley Forbes and Marilyn K. Smith

Chapter 1

Making Considerations

When working with learning disabled students, slow learners, remedial students or other at-risk students, many things need to be considered.

We will address a few considerations that we feel are the most important.

We have incorporated these in our classroom to make *all* students successful.

Classroom Environment

The first consideration is the classroom environment.

It needs to be student-friendly. Besides the obvious external motivators, such as bulletin boards, displaying student work and motivational posters, other factors need to be considered as important. The classroom must provide opportunities for the child to feel safe in taking risks. This can be established by providing successes early in the year for each individual child. A child needs to feel that any response given in the classroom makes a positive contribution to the learning process.

Children need to be allowed choice on a daily basis. Examples of choice may be as simple as deciding which center to go to, finding a cooperative group to interact with, or choosing a trade book to find notes on a particular subject for theme study. A more complex form of choice may include letting a child select a novel for literature study, or the whole class choosing which topics to study in a particular social studies or science theme.

We have found that a heterogeneous group is needed for students of all levels to be successful. This would include high, average and low-achieving students. Modeling by the students, as well as the teacher, is an important part of the learning process.

COURAGE

Courage is the strength to try something new.

With teamwork you can make

The Golden Rule

Treat others as you want to be treated.

Student's Learning Style

Another consideration that needs to be made is how each student learns most effectively.

A student's style of learning may be visual, auditory, kinesthetic, haptic or some combination. When looking at a student's style of learning, you must not only look at the input strengths but also the output/responding strengths. An output strength includes verbal, written or demonstration.

For some students to be successful in a regular classroom, you must modify the curriculum, instruction and tests. We have created a general form, Student Modification Checklist (page 9), and incorporate it in our classroom to help us match the student's learning style with the student's output. This is a constant reminder to us as the student's primary teachers, and it also benefits the child when he or she comes into contact with other teachers, such as music, physical education, art or a substitute teacher.

Types of Learning Styles

- An auditory learner is one who learns by listening. These types of students learn from verbal instruction. Often these learners need phonics in their instruction, talk while they write and/or are easily distracted by noise.

- A visual learner is one who learns by seeing and writing. These types of students learn by seeing words or pictures. These learners have vivid imaginations, think in pictures and use color.

- A kinesthetic learner is one who learns through large motor or whole body movements. These students learn by doing. They are impulsive, often poor spellers and not avid readers.

- A tactile learner is one who learns through small motor movements. They too learn by doing. They have many of the same traits as a kinesthetic learner.

Sample Student Modification Checklist

Student _____ Jacob Ikerd _____   Year/Grade _____ 4th _____

	First Quarter	Second Quarter	Third Quarter	Fourth Quarter
Curriculum Modifications				
Shorten assignments	✓	✓		
Use of math manipulatives with assignments (calculators, fact charts, etc.)	✓	✓	✓	✓
Supplementary materials				
Flexible time limits	✓	✓	✓	✓
Study guides	✓	✓		
Graphic organizers	✓	✓	✓	✓
Demonstrating			✓	
Illustrating	✓	✓		
Variety of types of tasks	✓	✓		
Reteach content				
Instruction Adaptations				
Independent activities				
Small group activities			✓	
Cooperative activities	✓	✓		
Whole class activities				✓
Material read orally	✓	✓	✓	
Material taped				
Highlight essential material	✓	✓	✓	✓
Individual assistance	✓	✓	✓	✓
Manipulatives	✓	✓	✓	✓
A-V materials				
Test Adaptations				
Read tests orally	✓	✓	✓	
Flexible time limits	✓	✓	✓	✓
Multiple choice				
Short answer				
Written essay				
Test key concepts only	✓	✓	✓	✓
Demonstration				
Oral reports	✓	✓		
Use of math manipulatives (calculators, fact charts, number line, etc.)	✓	✓	✓	✓

8

Student Modification Checklist

Student _____   Year/Grade _____

	First Quarter	Second Quarter	Third Quarter	Fourth Quarter
Curriculum Modifications				
Shorten assignments				
Use of math manipulatives with assignments (calculators, fact charts, etc.)				
Supplementary materials				
Flexible time limits				
Study guides				
Graphic organizers				
Demonstrating				
Illustrating				
Variety of types of tasks				
Reteach content				
Instruction Adaptations				
Independent activities				
Small group activities				
Cooperative activities				
Whole class activities				
Material read orally				
Material taped				
Highlight essential material				
Individual assistance				
Manipulatives				
A-V materials				
Test Adaptations				
Read tests orally				
Flexible time limits				
Multiple choice				
Short answer				
Written essay				
Test key concepts only				
Demonstration				
Oral reports				
Use of math manipulatives (calculators, fact charts, number line, etc.)				

Task/Assignment

The next consideration entails the task or assignment the student is asked to complete. Several points need to be addressed.

The first point is the factor of time. Setting a time limit can be detrimental to the successful completion of the task for some students. These students are so engrossed with the factor of time that the assignment is no longer a priority. For example, during a 50-minute writing assignment, an at-risk child may worry for the first 10 minutes about the time limit versus actually starting the assignment. When he actually gets down to completing the task, half or more of the time is over and the task is never completed. We do not advocate eliminating time lines, however, just time limits. (See page 20.)

The second point is the way students are asked to respond, for example: written or oral. For most students, the writing part of an assignment is an associative task. Writing each letter is an associative task while the thought is a cognitive task. For some students, the writing part of the assignment is also a cognitive task. These students are concentrating on how to write each letter as well as the thought. Thus, they are trying to complete two cognitive tasks at once. Think about this example:

- A teacher asks the students to take notes on vertebrates. While most students are concentrating on the information given about vertebrates, Josh is still trying to visualize what a cursive "v" looks like.

For other students, a task of answering a question verbally can be difficult. The problem here may be the pace of the questioning. A teacher asks a number of questions, randomly calling on students. For some students, the pace of the questioning is too rapid. The teacher may have moved onto the second question while these students are still processing the first question. Read the following example:

- The teacher asks, "Who was the first President of the United States?" Jacob answers, "George Washington." The teacher then asks, "Who is the current President of the United States?" Suzy is called upon and answers, "George Washington." Suzy was still processing the first question and never heard Jacob's reply or the second question.

TLC10111 Copyright © Teaching & Learning Company, Carthage, IL 62321-0010

A third point is the length of the assignment. The emphasis should be placed on the certain task you want the child to understand or master. Here are some examples.

- A teacher asks the students to complete a 10-page research paper on a Native American tribe including such topics as location, customs, diet, housing and clothing. A student might look at the task of 10 pages, feel overwhelmed with the length of the assignment and give up. Instead, the teacher could give this student the same assignment in steps. The student would be allowed to find specific information on each topic, and then compile the research paper.

- A teacher tells the students they will have a test on chapter 12 on Wednesday. This leaves the students responsible for all the information in that chapter. A better way would be to supply the students with a study guide emphasizing the specific material the teacher will be testing before starting the actual chapter.

A fourth point to consider is the technique of Model, Prompt and Practice. With any new instruction, this technique should be used. Modeling not only includes the teacher explaining the task to be done, but actually modeling the response wanted from the student. Students are watching, at this step not interacting. For example, the teacher wants the students to compare fractions. She talks through the process as she demonstrates multiple problems. Prompting involves the teacher and students. The teacher now starts the process of comparing two fractions. The students contribute as the process continues, with the help of the teacher when needed. Practicing is the next step. Students are given the actual assignment to complete. The teacher is now the facilitator. Model, Prompt and Practice should be incorporated in all subject areas.

Support

Support is desirable for both the teachers and the students.

It is essential when working with at-risk students. The teachers need to be able to collaborate and share ideas with other teachers. This could include the learning disabilities teacher, remedial reading teacher, speech teacher, language teacher, remedial math teacher or other teachers of the same grade level or subject matter. If at any-time any of these teachers co-teach with each other, co-planning is a must.

Support is also a necessity for the student. Modifications must be made throughout the day for at-risk students, not in just one subject matter or at a certain time of the day. Classes should be heterogeneous. These at-risk students need models of high and average students in the classroom. Students not only model academics, but also the social and nonverbal communication that many at-risk students lack. For example:

- You may hear a teacher or student tell a child sarcastically, "I can tell you really took your time on this." The at-risk child may take this as a compliment instead of an insult. The child may not understand the hidden meaning or sarcasm.

- Have you seen a child act inappropriately at a school library? The student may be talking loudly, randomly pulling books off the shelf or flipping through a card catalog. The child inevitably gets in trouble with the librarian and is often asked, "Don't you know how to act in a library?" In reality the child has never been taught this social skill or, possibly, has not been in a room where other students have modeled correct behavior.

Student support and teacher support are important for the success of an at-risk child in a typical classroom. They are as important as the actual modifications and strategies in instruction.

Chapter 2

Teacher's Toolbox

An assortment of items, charts, graphs, etc., help in everyday instruction with all students, especially the low-achieving, at-risk students.

because   listen

We call these items the Teacher's Toolbox because they need to be readily available at all times and easily accessible.

Some of these tools can be placed in a basket so they can be moved throughout the classroom as the teacher moves to assist the students.

outside

Sample **Daily Planner**

Student Name _____
Cody Bollin   Date ___7/23/97___

Reading
Roll of Thunder, Hear My Cry: pp. 68-74
Brady: pp. 70-79
  1. Find two new vocabulary words and define.
  2. Make a character sketch. Remember color and at least five characteristics.
  3. Find figurative language and illustrate.
  4. Respond.

Language/Writing
Begin prewriting of fairy tale using your graphic organizer.

Spelling
Find your words for the week. Take a list home to study. Test on Friday.

Social Studies/Science
Pioneer wagon due Monday. Gather supplies for the trip in groups.

Math
Review angles using clocks. Finding coordinates: pp. 71-72 in book. Use your graph paper.

Parent Note
Reminder: Awards assembly is Thursday at 10:00 a.m. Hope to see you there!

CHART

GRIDS

Teacher's Toolbox

Other items are kept in file folders in a box nearby to be used by students and teachers at a moment's notice.

Highlighters

Highlighters of all colors are used daily in our classroom.

They can be used when taking notes. Initially, teachers can assist the students in highlighting the important or main ideas. As this technique is modeled many times, it later becomes a strategy that is part of a child's routine. Highlighters can also be used for cues for starting, stopping and directionality. A child or teacher highlights green for "start" and red for "stop" in a number of situations such as the beginning of a line, margin, word, number or letter.

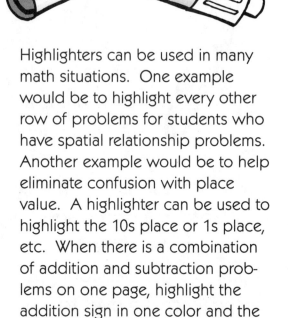

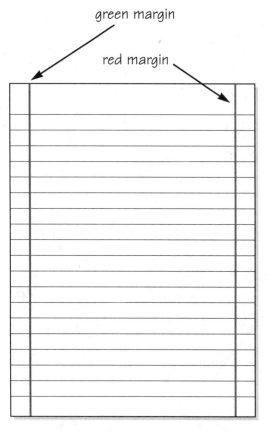

green margin

red margin

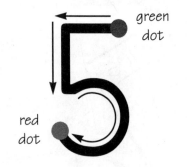

green dot

red dot

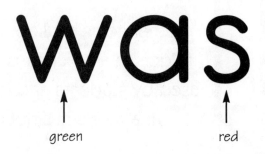

green   red

Highlighters can be used in many math situations. One example would be to highlight every other row of problems for students who have spatial relationship problems. Another example would be to help eliminate confusion with place value. A highlighter can be used to highlight the 10s place or 1s place, etc. When there is a combination of addition and subtraction problems on one page, highlight the addition sign in one color and the subtraction sign in another color. When working in division, highlighting the divisor or the dividend helps students who are easily confused.

Written directions can be confusing and lengthy to some students. Highlighting the key words in the directions helps the students to correctly complete the task. When using graphic organizers, students can highlight the part of the organizer they have used to complete the actual writing piece. When revising a story, students can highlight words or sections they wish to revise. Highlighting can be used when creating poems to show students where rhyming words should be located.

14

Multiplication/Addition Charts

Students should have access to multiplication and/or addition charts when appropriate. For example, a child could use a multiplication chart to help with the facts when doing long division.

Addition/Subtraction Fact Table

±	0	1	2	3	4	5	6	7	8	9
0	0	1	2	3	4	5	6	7	8	9
1	1	2	3	4	5	6	7	8	9	10
2	2	3	4	5	6	7	8	9	10	11
3	3	4	5	6	7	8	9	10	11	12
4	4	5	6	7	8	9	10	11	12	13
5	5	6	7	8	9	10	11	12	13	14
6	6	7	8	9	10	11	12	13	14	15
7	7	8	9	10	11	12	13	14	15	16
8	8	9	10	11	12	13	14	15	16	17
9	9	10	11	12	13	14	15	16	17	18

Multiplication/Division Fact Table

X÷	1	2	3	4	5	6	7	8	9	10
1	1	2	3	4	5	6	7	8	9	10
2	2	4	6	8	10	12	14	16	18	20
3	3	6	9	12	15	18	21	24	27	30
4	4	8	12	16	20	24	28	32	36	40
5	5	10	15	20	25	30	35	40	45	50
6	6	12	18	24	30	36	42	48	54	60
7	7	14	21	28	35	42	49	56	63	70
8	8	16	24	32	40	48	56	64	72	80
9	9	18	27	36	45	54	63	72	81	90
10	10	20	30	40	50	60	70	80	90	100

Math Grids

Math grids can be used for students with spatial relationship problems such as aligning math problems and place value.

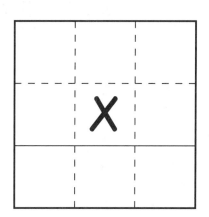

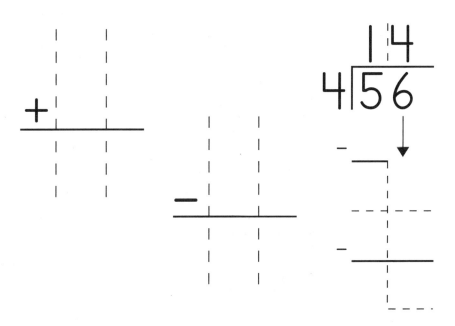

Place Value Charts

Place value charts enable the lower-achieving child to complete assignments the same as other students in the same time frame. They can be helpful for the low-achiever until the child understands place value.

trillions			billions			millions			thousands					ones
hundred trillions	ten trillions	trillions	hundred billions	ten billions	billions	hundred millions	ten millions	millions	hundred thousands	ten thousands	thousands	hundreds	tens	ones

tens	ones	.	tenths	hundredths	thousandths
1	4	.	4	3	7

thousandths	0.001s	10^{-3}
hundredths	0.01s	10^{-2}
tenths	0.1s	10^{-1}
.	.	.
ones	1s	10^{0}
tens	10s	10^{1}
hundreds	100s	10^{2}
thousands	1000s	10^{3}
ten thousands	10,000s	10^{4}
hundred thousands	100,000s	10^{5}
millions	1,00,000s	10^{6}
10M		10^{7}
100M		10^{8}
billions	1000 millions	10^{9}
10B		10^{10}
100B		10^{11}
trillions	1000 billions	10^{12}

Classroom Charts

Classroom charts can cover anything from school rules to the writing process. Others may include:

- checklists
- multiplication charts
- flow charts
- parts of speech
- punctuation
- capitalization
- proofreading marks
- literature genres
- writing components
- alphabet charts
- definitions of key terms
- graphic organizers

These charts are daily reminders to the children who have short-term memory deficits. These students can use their time appropriately on the assignment rather than on the format. The charts should be at students' eye level and visible by all. Charts should be changed to meet the individual growth of the students throughout the year.

Writing Process

1. Prewriting
2. Drafting
3. Revising
4. Editing
5. Final Draft

Timer

A timer in the classroom can be very beneficial. For an auditory learner, the ticking of the timer reminds the student that he or she should stay on task until the time period has ended. The timer can also be used in individual writing conferences. The teacher sets the timer for two minutes to ask for clarifications, solve problems, brainstorm or edit with the teacher. When the two minutes are finished, the teacher and timer move on to the next student. For the child who is in constant motion, the timer can be used to alternate between out-of-seat tasks and in-seat tasks. For visual learners, a sand-filled two-minute timer would be more beneficial.

Clipboard

A clipboard can assist a poorly coordinated and/or disorganized student. The clipboard holds papers for students who frequently lose papers off their desks. It can organize papers for a student's research project. It keeps the student's papers in one place. The clipboard can be kept on the corner of the desk or table or hooked on the side of the desk.

Graph Paper

Graph paper can be used in many ways:
- working with coordinates
- aligning addition, subtraction and multiplication problems
- organizing long division

When working with place value, the graph paper can be counted and cut to make place value blocks. In spelling, a student can write spelling words on graph paper to show the length of the word and to differentiate between the letters.

Skill Cards

Display cards in the classroom to remind students of basic skills. In literature, you might use index cards with one skill written on each card such as:
- setting
- characterization
- cause and effect
- sequence
- etc.

When asking students daily to respond in a literature log, the visible cues help them construct meaningful responses using learned skills. This may also be done in language/writing. Cards such as verbs, nouns, compound sentences, fables, poems, etc., can be displayed. Or use cards to display a math skill or lesson. You'll no longer hear students saying, "We haven't been taught that." An added benefit is the parents and administrators who glance in your room will see that the basics *are* being taught!

Setting

Characterization

Cause and Effect

Sequence

Word Lists

There are two types of word lists. The first type is a word list of specific purposes which you might find in a published book. The second type is created by the teacher and students and is continually added to throughout the year. This could be a list of words compiled to take the place of the word *said*. Another example could be a list of descriptive words to be used for a special piece of writing.

CHART

alive   cross
be   strong
speechless
exhausted
funny
tired
unsure
blue

Descriptive Words

This list of descriptive words was developed with our students for use in writing cinquain poems.

alive	bold	brainy	brave	courageous	curious
capable	cautious	clever	competent	energetic	fearless
aggressive	annoyed	arrogant	callous	cross	defiant
daring	determined	durable	eager	heavy	heroic
firm	forceful	gallant	cranky	inquisitive	lively
envious	gentle	hardy	healthy	impatient	insensitive
important	influential	innocent	intense	outstanding	powerful
fierce	furious	harsh	hostile	skillful	mean
intolerant	lucky	manly	mighty	strong	tame
relaxed	robust	secure	shy	vicious	violent
obnoxious	repulsive	spirited	stable	bored	bewildered
zealous	rude	spiteful	tense	bashful	dangerous
wicked	alone	awful	blue	helpless	discouraged
clumsy	confused	afraid	anxious	gloomy	embarrassed
depressed	dismal	doubtful	foolish	jealous	distrustful
fearful	frantic	hesitant	horrified	silly	skeptical
hopeless	lonely	lonesome	impatient	sad	overwhelmed
jumpy	nervous	puzzled	ridiculous	troubled	uncomfortable
speechless	panicky	scared	unhappy	timid	uneasy
tearful	terrible	tired	brilliant	calm	cheerful
unlucky	unpopular	unsure	admired	caring	charming
cowardly	amused	blissful	frail	excellent	fantastic
comical	delighted	ecstatic	glad	cooperative	courteous
charitable	exhausted	fragile	busy	careful	
fit	funny	considerate	concerned	confident	

Organizational Time Lines

At-risk students have trouble organizing and completing a long-term project on time. An organizational time line alleviates this problem. It consists of a checklist of the tasks to be completed with an individual date by each task. This breaks up the long-term project into achievable smaller tasks, enabling students to see all the steps needed to complete the whole project. It also keeps a student from procrastinating until the last minute.

Animal Unit Time Line

Research/Locate Info.	4/25/98	_____
Note Cards	5/11/98	_____
Rough Draft	5/98	_____
Peer Edit	98	_____
Final Copy	8	_____
Project Ho		

Colored Index Cards

Colored index cards can be used in a variety of ways:
- reading marker
- color code subject cards
- highlight information

They can be used to color code note cards and information when writing notes on a particular subject. Each color can represent a different subtopic. When a student finds information, it can be highlighted in a particular color and then transferred to the index card of the same color. Colored index cards come in a variety of sizes; a bigger size may help students who write large because of perceptual or motor difficulties.

Window Cards

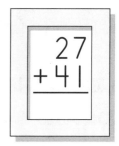

Window cards are made from tagboard or index cards. Cut a hole in the center of the card the size needed for the task. The hole in the card allows the student to focus on a reduced amount of material at a time. Keep different sizes of window cards available for use with reading and math. For example: in reading, one word or one line of text is exposed at a time. In math, one problem is revealed at a time.

he said | because | need you

L-Shaped Reading Guide

This is a large tagboard or index card cut into the shape of an *L*. The child who has left to right directionality problems moves the guide left to right as he or she reads. The card makes the child focus on one word or phrase at a time.

once | upon a time

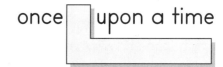

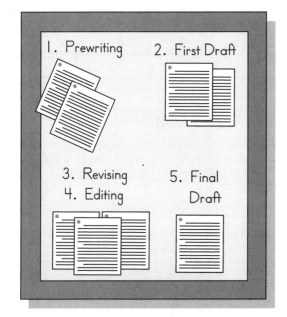

Scissors and Tape

Many students have trouble organizing the material in their writing assignments. How often have you seen a child write about three different topics in one paragraph? Or have you read a student's paper lately that had the ending in the middle? A simple way to help a child organize a paper is to have him or her write on one side of the paper only and skip lines. This allows you to help in the revision stage by cutting the paper and taping the sentences or paragraphs together in the correct sequence. The paper is ready to be made into a final copy, and the child only has to do one rewrite.

Daily Planners

A daily planner consists of a snapshot of what the day is going to entail.

The teacher fills out his or her plan for the day and makes a copy for each child. This allows students to see assignments for the day and also gives them a way to organize their day. You may not want to add entries other than assignments, such as: times for specific subjects (physical education, music, art, etc.) and parent notes to help communication from school to home. Send daily planners home every day to be shared with parents to show them what learning took place and what assignments need to be completed. Students may highlight any work that needs to be done. When students go home and are asked, "What did you do today at school?" they can show what took place.

Daily planners are especially beneficial when a student is absent. Often a parent calls or stops by at the end of the day for their child's work. The daily planner is easily accessible to the teacher. She can find the materials needed to go with the planner and highlight the work that needs to be completed. If a child does not receive the work ahead of time, then the planner is on their desk when they return showing the work that the child would need to make up.

Having the daily planner completed by the teacher allows the lower-achieving student to focus on the assignments rather than on writing down the assignments correctly. As the child matures and becomes more familiar with how the daily planner is completed, he or she can begin to complete some of the components.

Sample **Daily Planner**

Student Name _____Cody Bollin_____ Date __7/23/97__

Reading

Roll of Thunder, Hear My Cry: pp. 68-74
Brady: pp. 70-79

1. Find two new vocabulary words and define.
2. Make a character sketch. Remember color and at least five characteristics.
3. Find figurative language and illustrate.
4. Respond.

Language/Writing

Begin prewriting of fairy tale using your graphic organizer.

Spelling

Find your words for the week.
Take a list home to study. Test on Friday.

Social Studies/Science

Pioneer wagon due Monday.
Gather supplies for the trip in groups.

Math

Review angles using clocks.
Finding coordinates: pp. 71-72 in book.
Use your graph paper.

Parent Note

Reminder: Awards assembly is Thursday at 10:00 a.m. Hope to see you there!

Daily Planner

Student Name _____ Date _____

Reading

Language/Writing

Math

Social Studies/Science

Spelling

Parent Note

Student Name _____ Date _____

Reading

Language/Writing

Spelling

Math

Social Studies/
Science

Parent Note

Student Name _____ Date _____

Reading

_____

Spelling

_____

Social Studies/Science

_____

Language/Writing

_____

Math

_____

Parent Note

_____

Student Name _____ Date _____

Reading

Language/Writing

Math

Social Studies/Science

Spelling

Parent Note

Student Name _____ Date _____

Reading

_____

Spelling

_____

Social Studies/Science

_____

Language/Writing

_____

Math

_____

Parent Note

_____

Student Name _____ **Date** _____

Reading

Language/Writing

Spelling

Math

Social Studies/ Science

Parent Note

Mini Whiteboards

Many students have allergies. Because of this, individual chalkboards can cause problems. Cut a large whiteboard into smaller pieces to make individual practice boards. These help alleviate allergy problems and also allow for color coding during instruction and practice. Using mini whiteboards and dry-erase markers, students can respond to a question at the same time. No one can rely on another student's answer. The teacher can get a quick glance at the students' individual responses to help catch any mistakes. Mini whiteboards are motivating to the students and help them practice skills such as math, spelling, etc. Dry-erase eraser may be used or a sample of carpet can be cut into small individual pieces to be used as erasers. (Socks work, too.)

Static Paper

Static paper is a thin, white paper that works like a whiteboard but is easy to move. It sticks to almost any surface (even those awful brick walls found in many classrooms). Static paper allows for a quick surface for taking notes, making charts or lists, or making graphic organizers. Use dry-erase markers and erasers.

Whiteboards

The whiteboard we use is a marlite board. It can be found at any lumber store for approximately $15.00 per board. They come in 4' x 8' (1.2 x 2.4 m) sheets. You can get 32 12" x 12" student boards from a sheet this size. Some stores will even cut it for you

Static paper can be purchased or ordered at most school supply or business supply stores.

Penlight

A penlight or small flashlight can be used as a marker for students to follow as they read, thus highlighting or focusing on one word at a time. It is a motivator for students who do not want to use a window card or a finger. A penlight allows the teacher to quickly glance at the student's page to see if he or she is following along correctly. A teacher can also see the fluency rate of a child who is reading silently by watching the light move across the page.

Friendly Letter

Heading

Greeting

Body

Closing

Signature

Overhead Projector

Every classroom should have an overhead projector to allow every child to see the same thing at the same time. When teachers write on large chalkboards or whiteboards, only half of the class actually sees what he or she is writing. The half behind the teacher's back must wait until the writing is done to see it. It is especially important for the entire class to see when the teacher is showing a math process or teaching how to write a letter. There are other ways to use an overhead projector effectively. Make transparencies of worksheets on a copying machine. Color coding can be done on a transparency if a whiteboard is not available. Math manipulatives can be made from transparencies or bought at a local teacher supply store. Using an overhead projector allows for the Model, Prompt and Practice technique to take place. (See page 11.)

Chapter 3

Graphic Organizers and Rubrics

You may have learning disabled students, remedial reading and math students, at-risk students in your classroom, as well as, low-achieving students who do not fit under a particular label.

Your biggest challenge with all of these students is to get them to write!

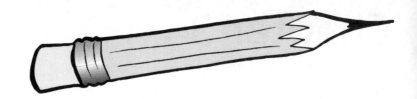

We have heard many times from teachers and administrators that low-achieving students are unable to write. We, too, struggled with this problem. Have you experienced a similar situation?

Imagine that it is the first day of new fallen snow and students and teachers alike are excited. You write a story starter on the board. "If you were a snowflake, how would you feel?" Many eager students begin writing, but your lowest-achieving student gives you a finished paper after a few minutes. His paper reads:
I am a snowflake. It got warm.
I melted. The end.

The child did include a beginning, a middle and an ending. However, no details were included in the story.

Many low-achieving students do not know what else to add to a story. Some will not even attempt to start, "Because," they say, "I don't know what to write." Others start with good intentions but are lost about what to do next.

We need to give these students more guidance and assistance. If, in the writing process, the step of prewriting was more detailed, these students would be able to write and organize a more complete and interesting story, holding his own against the "average" students. The low-achieving student begins to feel better about what she is writing and feels successful. The result is that these students become better writers and are more willing to write when asked to complete as assignment.

One of our fifth grade writing deficient students, Joe, hated to write and would let us know about it every day. Throughout the year, we encouraged his writing and provided him with prewriting graphic organizers for each writing piece we asked him to do. He soon realized that he could write if given some guidance on what to include and what to do next.

We did not know how much of an impact we had made on him and his writing until one spring day Joe came into the room very quietly, which was unlike him. He sat at his desk and began to write in a notebook. This was very unusual for Joe. We watched him for a few minutes and then continued with the normal morning activities. Joe continued to write, ignoring everything around him. Math began next, but Joe was still writing. We decided to let him write and ignored his nonparticipation in the math we were doing.

Later that day, Joe handed us his paper. He asked if we could type it and give it back to him. We had done this before for other writing pieces that we thought he had been proud of, so this was not an unusual request. But the story was very unusual for him. As you read his piece, you will notice that Joe turned to writing to comfort himself. As we cried reading this paper, we knew we had finally reached Joe and were successful.

We edited only for punctuation and spelling.

The Dog I Really Loved

It all started on a Thursday, January of 1994. This is how it goes. One day after school we went to my mom's friend's house out of town. We went there to get our new dog named J.D. When we got there we got to see J.D., our dog. We were about to leave when the lady started to cry. We hurried so she wouldn't change her mind about the dog.

When we got home, we showed the dog around. My sister took the dog for a walk to her friend's house. When she got home, J.D. wanted to eat my candy, so I gave him a bite. Then I took him outside to use the bathroom.

The next morning I called my friend Erik to see if he could play outside with his dog and mine. He could play, so his dog and mine went to the park to play. His dog didn't like me. I took J.D. home. One week later, we had to get rid of him because I had an infection in my arms. I've had allergies since I was six years old, so I had to get rid of him. My mom's friend wanted him, and I didn't want to get rid of him. But on Thursday the 10th, my mom took him to the lady's house. I cried because I didn't want to give it away. I cried on my mom's shoulder. Then I went to school. When I got home I was about to cry, but I kept up my strength so I would not cry. If my dog gets used to his new home, he can come to visit me. I love you, J.D., my favorite dog.

Graphic Organizers

Based on this success, we designed graphic organizers for each writing piece we asked students to write. We began designing rubrics to match the graphic organizers to help us better evaluate what it was we had asked students to write. Our evaluation of the students' writing became objective rather than subjective. Rubrics allow us to give points for the things we expect from students. The students know exactly what will be evaluated. They see the rubric before the writing assignment begins, so the assignment is not a guessing game. Sometimes students help make up the rubrics. Their input in the process is very valuable. Rubrics allow for fairness in evaluation for *all* students. Rubrics do not hinder the creativity of better writers because students are not limited to only the components required.

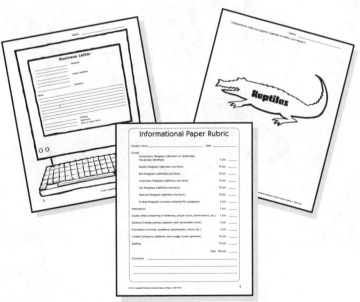

Use the following graphic organizers and rubrics. Adapt or revise them to suit your needs. Design your own graphic organizers and rubrics to meet the individual needs of your students. The best rule of thumb when designing rubrics is to weigh the content of the writing piece about 60% of the grade, and the context and mechanics the other 40% of the grade. This allows all students an opportunity to succeed. Following a few samples have been provided for you.

34

Name _____

Type of writing _____

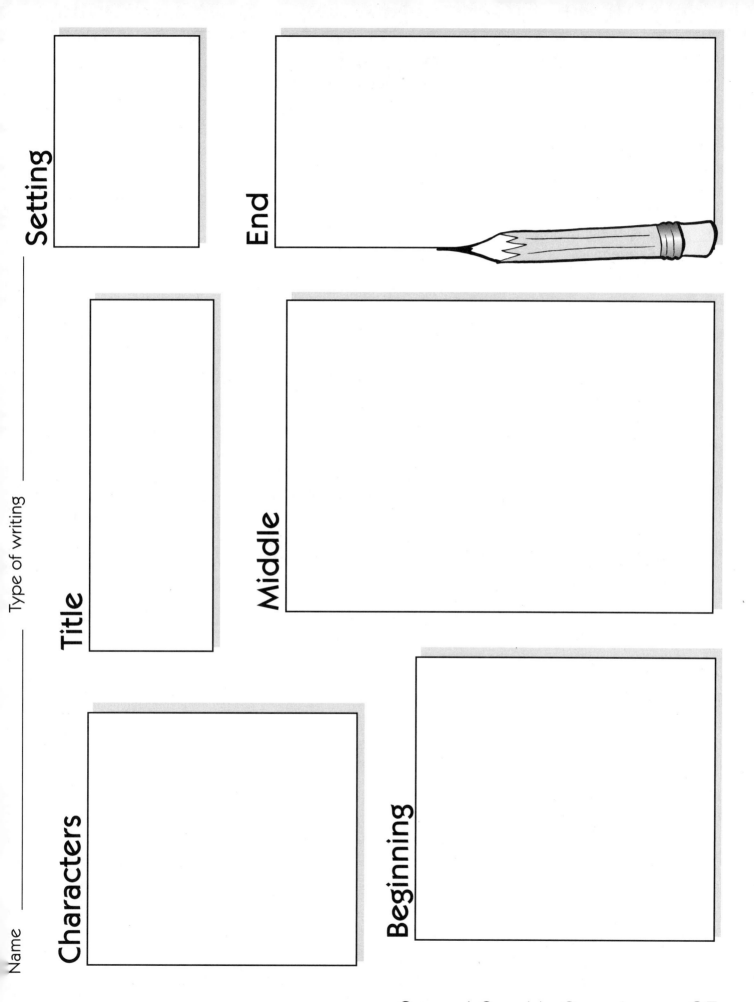

Setting

End

Title

Middle

Characters

Beginning

Rubric

Student Name _____ Date _____

Format
      Beginning, middle and end to the story   30 pts. _____
      Sequential

Main idea supported with descriptive details   30 pts. _____

Indentations   5 pts. _____

Capital Letters (beginning of sentences, proper nouns, abbreviations, etc.)   5 pts. _____

Sentence Endings (period, question mark, exclamation point)   5 pts. _____

Punctuation (commas, quotations, apostrophes, colons, etc.)   5 pts. _____

Context (omissions, additions, word usage, correct grammar)   10 pts. _____

Spelling   10 pts. _____

Total 100 pts. _____

Comments: _____

_____

_____

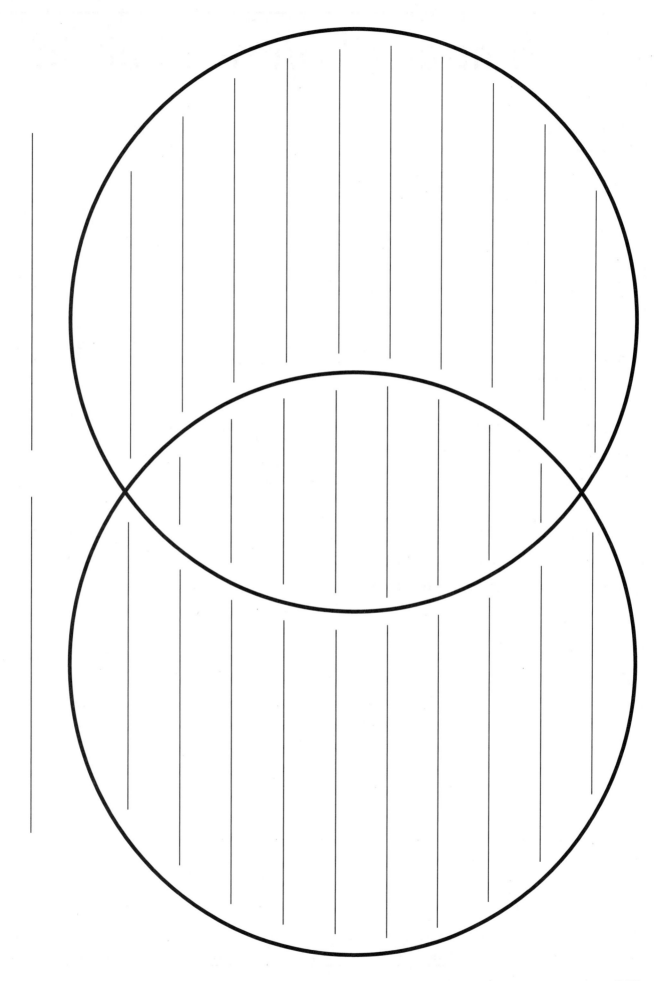

Compare/Contrast

Compare/Contrast Rubric

Student Name _____ Date _____

Format
    Factual information present   20 pts. _____

    Contrast   20 pts. _____

    Comparison   20 pts. _____

Indentations   5 pts. _____

Capital Letters (beginning of sentences, proper nouns, abbreviations, etc.)   5 pts. _____

Sentence Endings (period, question mark, exclamation point)   5 pts. _____

Punctuation (commas, quotations, apostrophes, colons, etc.)   5 pts. _____

Context (omissions, additions, word usage, correct grammar)   10 pts. _____

Spelling   10 pts. _____

                                            Total 100 pts. _____

Comments: _____

_____

_____

TLC10111 Copyright © Teaching & Learning Company, Carthage, IL 62321-0010

Personal Narrative Paper

Describe Yourself

age, eye color, hair color, size

Family

oldest, youngest, middle,
members in family, anything unique

Where You Live

city, town, state, in the country, in town,
describe your house

Hobbies

things you like to do, collections

Likes/Dislikes

food, sports, favorite teams, colors

Future

what you want to do, college, profession, marriage, kids

Write at least one paragraph for each topic.

Name _____

Personal Narrative

Describe Yourself

Family

Where You Live

Hobbies

Likes/Dislikes

Future

Personal Narrative Rubric

Student Name _____ Date _____

Format
    Topics included with *details*   60 pts. _____
        Description
        Family
        Home
        Hobbies
        Likes/Dislikes
        Future

Indentations   5 pts. _____

Capital Letters (beginning of sentences, proper nouns, abbreviations, etc.) 5 pts. _____

Sentence Endings (period, question mark, exclamation point)   5 pts. _____

Punctuation (commas, quotations, apostrophes, colons, etc.)   5 pts. _____

Context (omissions, additions, word usage, correct grammar)   10 pts. _____

Spelling   10 pts. _____

                                        Total 100 pts. _____

Comments: _____

_____

_____

Opinion Paper

Paragraph 1
State your opinion and three reasons why you believe that opinion.

Halloween is the best holiday to celebrate. Children of all ages are able to participate. Everyone is able to take many treats home. Dressing up each year in a different costume makes each year unique.

Paragraph 2
State your first reason and three statements that prove that reason.

Children of all ages are able to go trick-or-treating. Some are so young the parents have to carry them door to door. Others are experienced and able to go with a group of friends. No matter what age, they still have fun.

Paragraph 3
State your second reason and three statements that prove that reason.

_____

_____

_____

_____

Paragraph 4
State your third reason and three statements that prove that reason.

_____

_____

_____

Paragraph 5
State your opinion again, and restate your three reasons.

Halloween is the best of all holidays. All ages of children go trick-or-treating. Many treats are taken home by all. Each year a different costume makes each Halloween special.

Use to model with students.

Opinion Paper Outline

Paragraph 1 (opinion): _____

    First reason: _____

    Second reason: _____

    Third reason: _____

Paragraph 2 (first reason): _____

    A. _____

    B. _____

    C. _____

Paragraph 3 (second reason): _____

    A. _____

    B. _____

    C. _____

Paragraph 4 (third reason): _____

    A. _____

    B. _____

    C. _____

Paragraph 5 (restate the opinion): _____

    Restate first reason: _____

    Restate second reason: _____

    Restate third reason: _____

Opinion Paper Rubric

Student Name _____ Date _____

Format

    First paragraph states the opinion and three reasons.   20 pts. _____

    Body of the paper supports the three reasons.   20 pts. _____

    Ending paragraph restates the opinion and reasons.   20 pts. _____

Indentations   5 pts. _____

Capital Letters (beginning of sentences, proper nouns, abbreviations, etc.)   5 pts. _____

Sentence Endings (period, question mark, exclamation point)   5 pts. _____

Punctuation (commas, quotations, apostrophes, colons, etc.)   5 pts. _____

Context (omissions, additions, word usage, correct grammar)   10 pts. _____

Spelling   10 pts. _____

Total   100 pts. _____

Comments: _____

_____

_____

Name _____

Setting (describe)

Characters

Main character:

Supporting characters:

Fantasy

Identify the Problem

How Will Characters Deal with Their Problem?

Solution to the Problem

Fantasy Rubric

Student Name _____ Date _____

Format

    Character(s) descriptions   10 pts. _____

    Beginning, middle, ending   10 pts. _____

    Descriptive setting   10 pts. _____

    Identify the problem   10 pts. _____

    How the characters dealt with their problem   10 pts. _____

    Solution to the problem   10 pts. _____

Indentations   5 pts. _____

Capital Letters (beginning of sentences, proper nouns, abbreviations, etc.)   5 pts. _____

Sentence Endings (period, question mark, exclamation point)   5 pts. _____

Punctuation (commas, quotations, apostrophes, colons, etc.)   5 pts. _____

Context (omissions, additions, word usage, correct grammar)   10 pts. _____

Spelling   10 pts. _____

Total 100 pts. _____

Comments: _____

_____

What Is a Folktale?

A folktale conveys a certain truth about life or describes something that happens in nature.

The following components are found in most folktales:

- The beginning of the story starts with "Once upon a time . . ." or similar phrase.
- The story includes magic events, characters and objects.
- One character is someone of royalty (king, queen, prince, princess, etc.).
- One character is wicked.
- One character is good.
- Goodness is rewarded in the story.
- Certain numbers like *three* and *seven* are in the story.
- The story ends with " . . . they lived happily ever after."

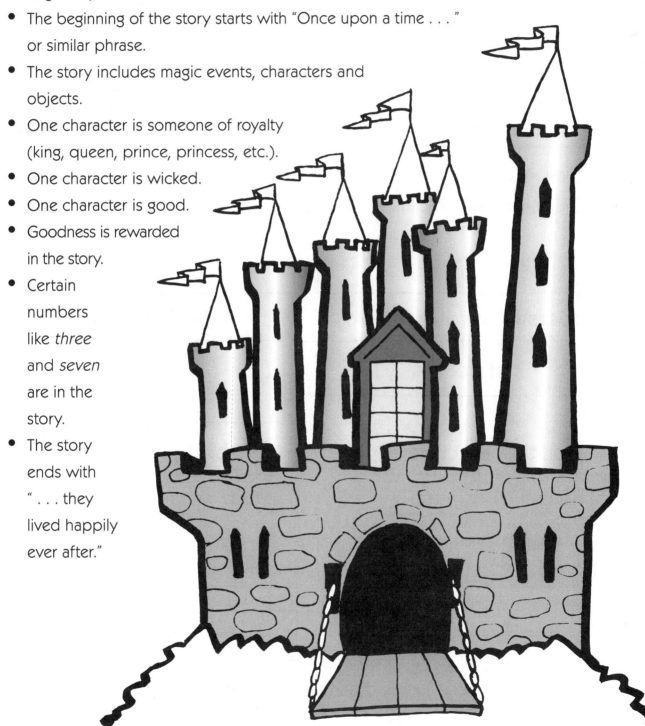

Teacher Note: Use to give background on the components of a folktale before using graphic organizer.

Sample

Folktale

Title

How Tinga Got Her Stripes

Story Beginning

A long, long time ago . . .

Magic

Stripes appear on Tinga's body

Royalty

King Lion

Numbers in the Story (3 or 7)

7 stripes

Wicked Characters

King Lion

Good Characters

Tinga, the tiger

Goodness Rewarded

first tiger to get stripes

Story Ending

King Lion gives all seven stripes to Tinga.
That is how the Tiger got its stripes.

Folktale

Title

Story Beginning

Magic

Royalty

Numbers in the Story (3 or 7)

Wicked Characters

Good Characters

Goodness Rewarded

Story Ending

Folktale Rubric

Sample

Student Name _____ *Bobby Jordan* _____ Date _____ *4/26/98* _____

Format

Story Beginning (Once upon a time, etc.)	5 pts.	*5*
Characters		
Royalty (king, queen, prince, princess, etc.)	5 pts.	*5*
Wicked Character(s)	5 pts.	*5*
Good Character(s)	5 pts.	*5*
Magic (events, characters or objects)	10 pts.	*10*
Goodness Rewarded	10 pts.	*10*
Certain Numbers (3 or 7)	5 pts.	*5*
Plot *(some confusing)*	10 pts.	*8*
Story Ending	5 pts.	*5*
Indentations ✔	5 pts.	*4*
Capital Letters (beginning of sentences, proper nouns, abbreviations, etc.) ✔	5 pts.	*4*
Sentence Endings (period, question mark, exclamation point) ✔	5 pts.	*4*
Punctuation (commas, quotations, apostrophes, colons, etc.)	5 pts.	*5*
Context (omissions, additions, word usage, correct grammar) ✔✔	10 pts.	*8*
Spelling	10 pts.	*8*

excited
loyalty

Total 100 pts. *91% B*

Comments: *Great story! Lots of details and well thought out!*

Folktale Rubric

Student Name _____ Date _____

Format

    Story Beginning (Once upon a time, etc.)   5 pts. _____

    Characters

        Royalty (king, queen, prince, princess, etc.)   5 pts. _____

        Wicked Character(s)   5 pts. _____

        Good Character(s)   5 pts. _____

    Magic (events, characters or objects)   10 pts. _____

    Goodness Rewarded   10 pts. _____

    Certain Numbers (3 or 7)   5 pts. _____

    Plot   10 pts. _____

    Story Ending   5 pts. _____

Indentations   5 pts. _____

Capital Letters (beginning of sentences, proper nouns, abbreviations, etc.) 5 pts. _____

Sentence Endings (period, question mark, exclamation point)   5 pts. _____

Punctuation (commas, quotations, apostrophes, colons, etc.)   5 pts. _____

Context (omissions, additions, word usage, correct grammar)   10 pts. _____

Spelling   10 pts. _____

                                    Total 100 pts. _____

Comments: _____

_____

_____

Name _____

Mystery of Nature
(Example: How do we get lightning?
Why are there volcanoes?)

God(s) (traits)

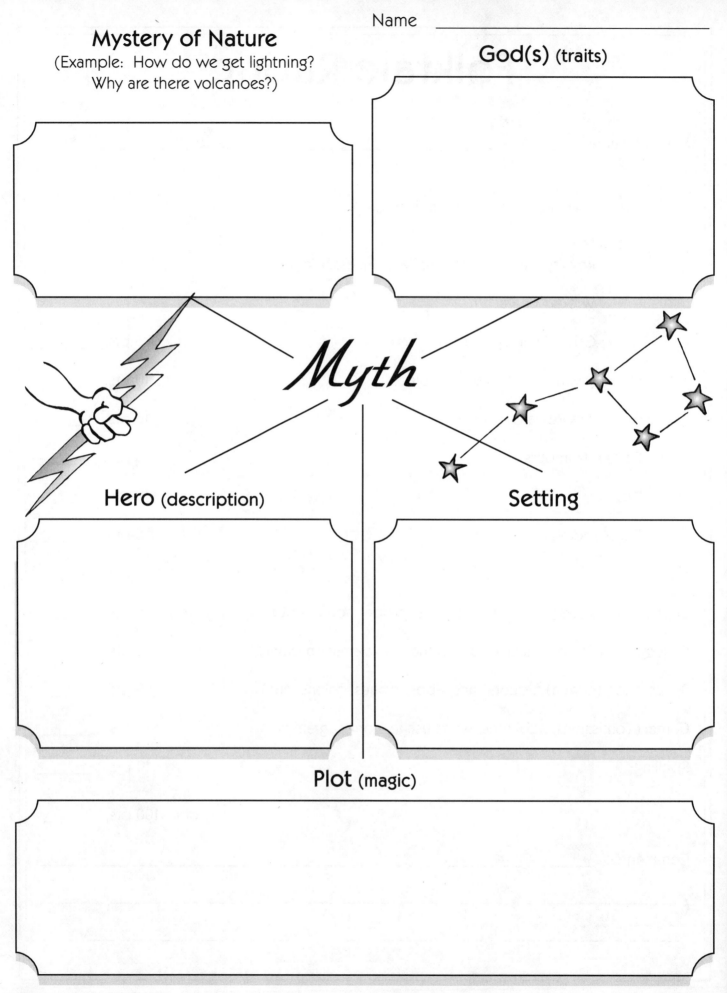

Myth

Hero (description)

Setting

Plot (magic)

Myth Rubric

Student Name _____   Date _____

Format

    Mystery of Nature   10 pts. _____

    Characters–(hero, god[s])   10 pts. _____

    Setting   10 pts. _____

    Plot (magic)   10 pts. _____

    Beginning, Middle and Ending to the Story   20 pts. _____

Indentations   5 pts. _____

Capital Letters (beginning of sentences, proper nouns, abbreviations, etc.)   5 pts. _____

Sentence Endings (period, question mark, exclamation point)   5 pts. _____

Punctuation (commas, quotations, apostrophes, colons, etc.)   5 pts. _____

Context (omissions, additions, word usage, correct grammar)   10 pts. _____

Spelling   10 pts. _____

Total   100 pts. _____

Comments: _____

_____

_____

Name _____

Mystery

Detective/Crime Solver

Problem/Crime

Solution to the Crime

Setting

Motive

Good Guys

Possible Suspects

Clues

1.

2.

3.

Mystery Rubric

Student Name _____   Date _____

Format

    Beginning, Middle, Ending   15 pts. _____

    Detective/Crime Solver   5 pts. _____

    Setting   5 pts. _____

    Good Guys   5 pts. _____

    Possible Suspects   5 pts. _____

    Clues (minimum of three)   9 pts. _____

    Problem/Crime   5 pts. _____

    Solution to the Crime   5 pts. _____

    Motive   6 pts. _____

Indentations   5 pts. _____

Capital Letters (beginning of sentences, proper nouns, abbreviations, etc.)   5 pts. _____

Sentence Endings (period, question mark, exclamation point)   5 pts. _____

Punctuation (commas, quotations, apostrophes, colons, etc.)   5 pts. _____

Context (omissions, additions, word usage, correct grammar)   10 pts. _____

Spelling   10 pts. _____

                                              Total   100 pts. _____

Comments: _____

_____

_____

Fairy Tale

Beginning Words	Magic Event/Character

and/or

Royal Character(s)	Animal Character(s)

Evil Character(s)	Special Number

Lesson	Ending Words

Fairy Tale Rubric

Student Name _____ Date _____

Format

      Beginning Words   5 pts. _____

      Magic Event/Character   10 pts. _____

      Royal Character(s) and/or Animal Character(s)   5 pts. _____

      Evil Character(s)   5 pts. _____

      Special Number   10 pts. _____

      Lesson   20 pts. _____

      Ending Words   5 pts. _____

Indentations   5 pts. _____

Capital Letters (beginning of sentences, proper nouns, abbreviations, etc.)   5 pts. _____

Sentence Endings (period, question mark, exclamation point)   5 pts. _____

Punctuation (commas, quotations, apostrophes, colons, etc.)   5 pts. _____

Context (omissions, additions, word usage, correct grammar)   10 pts. _____

Spelling   10 pts. _____

Total   100 pts. _____

Comments: _____

_____

_____

Characters

Setting (woods or countryside)

Fable

What Happens in the Plot

Lesson or Moral

Remember to use personification in your story.

Fable Rubric

Student Name _____ Date _____

Format

    Beginning, Middle, Ending   25 pts. _____

    Characters (animals or forces of nature)   5 pts. _____

    Setting (woods or countryside)   5 pts. _____

    Plot (involves one or two characters)   10 pts. _____

    Lesson or Moral   5 pts. _____

    Personification   10 pts. _____

Indentations   5 pts. _____

Capital Letters (beginning of sentences, proper nouns, abbreviations, etc.)   5 pts. _____

Sentence Endings (period, question mark, exclamation point)   5 pts. _____

Punctuation (commas, quotations, apostrophes, colons, etc.)   5 pts. _____

Context (omissions, additions, word usage, correct grammar)   10 pts. _____

Spelling   10 pts. _____

                                       Total   100 pts. _____

Comments: _____

_____

_____

Tall Tale

A tall tale is a story that stretches the truth about the character, plot or setting.

Make up a character to write a tall tale about. Answer the questions below and on the following page to help you.

1. What is your character's name? _____

2. Name five special things about your character (use descriptive words). Then turn them into exaggerations.

a. _____ — _____

_____

_____

b. _____ — _____

_____

_____

c. _____ — _____

_____

_____

d. _____ — _____

_____

_____

e. _____ — _____

_____

_____

Tall Tale (continued)

3. Where does the story take place? _____

_____

_____

4. Tell in short phrases or sentences things that will happen in your story.

_____

_____

_____

_____

_____

_____

_____

_____

_____

_____

_____

_____

Tall Tale Rubric

Student Name _____ Date _____

Format
    Beginning, Middle, Ending   30 pts. _____

    Characters Descriptions, Setting   10 pts. _____

    Five Exaggerations   20 pts. _____

Indentations   5 pts. _____

Capital Letters (beginning of sentences, proper nouns, abbreviations, etc.)   5 pts. _____

Sentence Endings (period, question mark, exclamation point)   5 pts. _____

Punctuation (commas, quotations, apostrophes, colons, etc.)   5 pts. _____

Context (omissions, additions, word usage, correct grammar)   10 pts. _____

Spelling   10 pts. _____

                                              Total   100 pts. _____

Comments: _____

_____

_____

Sample

Historical Fiction

Historical Fiction Title	Edward's Dream of Land
Choose a Historical Period/Event	Medieval Times
Setting	Castle and manor in England
Main Character (real or made up)	Edward
Other Characters	Edward's father, Edward's uncle

List of Happenings
(during this historical period)

feudalism
manorialism
knighthood*
tournament*
banquet*
falconry and
  hunting
crusades*

*use in story

Main Action
(believable)

Edward—second
  son of lord
Edward becoming
  a knight
Steps:
1. page—8 years old
2. squire—15/16
   years old
3. knight—20 years
   old
Tournament or
  war games
(Edward is winner,
won war-horse,
won purse of gold)
Banquet—food,
  music, dancers

Story Scenes

Edward—second son
  of lord, wants to
  become a knight
Goes to Uncle's
  castle for training
Becomes a knight
Tournament—war is
  over with
  crusades
Banquet—celebrates
  winning tourna-
  ment presented
  with his own piece
  of land

Historical Fiction

Historical Fiction Title

Choose a Historical Period/Event

Setting

Main Character (real or made up)

Other Characters

List of Happenings (during this historical period)	Main Action (believable)	Story Scenes

Sample

Historical Fiction Rubric

Student Name ___Marcus Whewell___   Date ___11/5/98___

Format

Setting	5 pts.	_5_
Main Character Description (real or made up)	5 pts.	_5_
Happenings (during historical period)	15 pts.	_15_
Main Action (believable)	10 pts.	_10_
Sequential Story Scenes	10 pts.	_10_
Beginning, Middle, Ending	15 pts.	_15_

Indentations   5 pts.   _5_

Capital Letters (beginning of sentences, proper nouns, abbreviations, etc.)   5 pts.   _2_

✓   ✓✓

Sentence Endings (period, question mark, exclamation point)   5 pts.   _4_

⊙

Punctuation (commas, quotations, apostrophes, colons, etc.)   5 pts.   _3_

^   *father's*

Context (omissions, additions, word usage, correct grammar)   10 pts.   _10_

Spelling   10 pts.   _8_

medieval

tournament   Total 100 pts. *92% A*

Comments: _Good story plot, well-thought out details_

_____

_____

Historical Fiction Rubric

Student Name _____   Date _____

Format

    Setting   5 pts. _____

    Main Character Description (real or made up)   5 pts. _____

    Happenings (during historical period)   15 pts. _____

    Main Action (believable)   10 pts. _____

    Sequential Story Scenes   10 pts. _____

    Beginning, Middle, Ending   15 pts. _____

Indentations   5 pts. _____

Capital Letters (beginning of sentences, proper nouns, abbreviations, etc.)   5 pts. _____

Sentence Endings (period, question mark, exclamation point)   5 pts. _____

Punctuation (commas, quotations, apostrophes, colons, etc.)   5 pts. _____

Context (omissions, additions, word usage, correct grammar)   10 pts. _____

Spelling   10 pts. _____

Total   100 pts. _____

Comments: _____

_____

TLC10111 Copyright © Teaching & Learning Company, Carthage, IL 62321-0010

Realistic Fiction

Choose a way to begin your story.
1. Dialogue
2. Question
3. Description
4. Background information
5. Main character introducing himself/herself

Setting (be specific)

Characters (be specific)

Story Scenes (main actions)

Problem (must be realistic)

Dialogue
* Remember to use dialogue
* Follow the rules
  - begin new paragraph when new person speaks
  - use quotations
  - avoid overuse of word *said*

Effective Closing (problem solved or overcome)

Purpose (serious, scary, funny, surprising, sad)

Realistic Fiction Rubric

Student Name _____ Date _____

Format

    Story Beginning   5 pts. _____

    Setting   5 pts. _____

    Problem   10 pts. _____

    Story Scenes
        (used specific details, allowed audience to see the action)   10 pts. _____

    Purpose   10 pts. _____

    Effective Closing   10 pts. _____

    Dialogue (correct use of quotations)   10 pts. _____

Indentations   5 pts. _____

Capital Letters (beginning of sentences, proper nouns, abbreviations, etc.)   5 pts. _____

Sentence Endings (period, question mark, exclamation point)   5 pts. _____

Punctuation (commas, quotations, apostrophes, colons, etc.)   5 pts. _____

Context (omissions, additions, word usage, correct grammar)   10 pts. _____

Spelling   10 pts. _____

                                          Total   100 pts. _____

Comments: _____

_____

_____

Two Bad Ants
Writing Assignment

One morning two ants went out on a journey. They moved through many wild places. Suddenly they found themselves in a very unfamiliar place.

Use the passage above to start your story about two bad ants. Describe at least three different experiences the ants had on their adventure. Think of the examples in the real book: coffee cup, toaster, faucet, disposal.

Remember: Do not tell the reader what the object is that you are describing. Only describe what it looks and feels like to the ants. Let the reader figure out the object through your description and illustrations.

Good luck!

To be used with the book *Two Bad Ants* by Chris Van Allsburg.

Two Bad Ants
Story Map

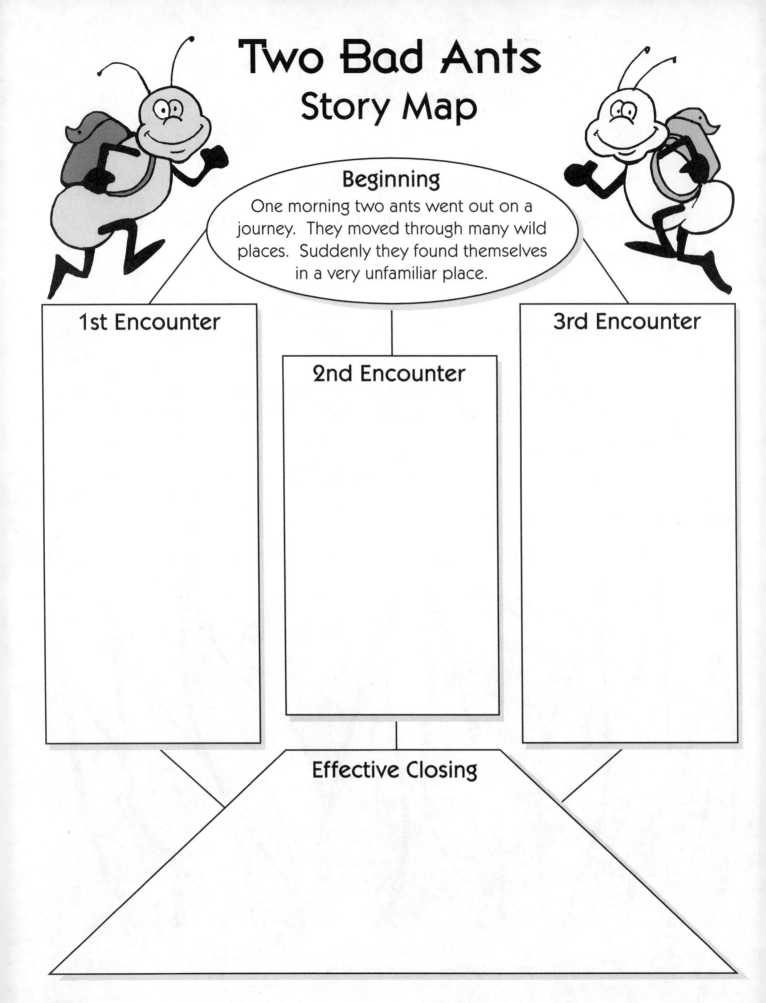

Beginning

One morning two ants went out on a journey. They moved through many wild places. Suddenly they found themselves in a very unfamiliar place.

1st Encounter

2nd Encounter

3rd Encounter

Effective Closing

TLC10111 Copyright © Teaching & Learning Company, Carthage, IL 62321-0010

Two Bad Ants Rubric

Student Name _____ Date _____

Format
> Paper describes at least three experiences the
> ants had without telling the actual object   20 pts. _____

Illustrations
> Helped the audience understand the story with
> the visuals used to describe the experiences   20 pts. _____

Story Beginning, Middle, Ending   20 pts. _____

Indentations   5 pts. _____

Capital Letters (beginning of sentences, proper nouns, abbreviations, etc.)   5 pts. _____

Sentence Endings (period, question mark, exclamation point)   5 pts. _____

Punctuation (commas, quotations, apostrophes, colons, etc.)   5 pts. _____

Context (omissions, additions, word usage, correct grammar)   10 pts. _____

Spelling   10 pts. _____

Total   100 pts. _____

Comments: _____

_____

_____

Name _____

DINOSAUR
Research Paper

Habitat

Description

Dinosaur Name

Enemies

Size

Food

OUTLINE FOR DINOSAUR RESEARCH PAPER

Paragraph 1   Introduction

Paragraph 2   Habitat

Paragraph 3   Description

Paragraph 4   Size

Paragraph 5   Food

Paragraph 6   Enemies

Paragraph 7   Interesting facts

Paragraph 8   Effective closing

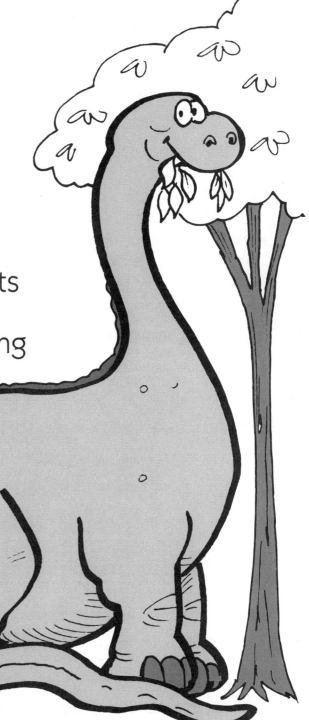

Dinosaur Research Paper Rubric

Student Name _____ Date _____

Format
    Habitat (where they lived and/or period)   10 pts. _____

      Description   15 pts. _____

      Size (weight, length, height)   15 pts. _____

      Food   10 pts. _____

      Enemies   10 pts. _____

Indentations   5 pts. _____

Capital Letters (beginning of sentences, proper nouns, abbreviations, etc.) 5 pts. _____

Sentence Endings (period, question mark, exclamation point)   5 pts. _____

Punctuation (commas, quotations, apostrophes, colons, etc.)   5 pts. _____

Context (omissions, additions, word usage, correct grammar)   10 pts. _____

Spelling   10 pts. _____

                                           Total 100 pts. _____

Comments: _____

_____

_____

Vertebrate Research Paper

Name _____

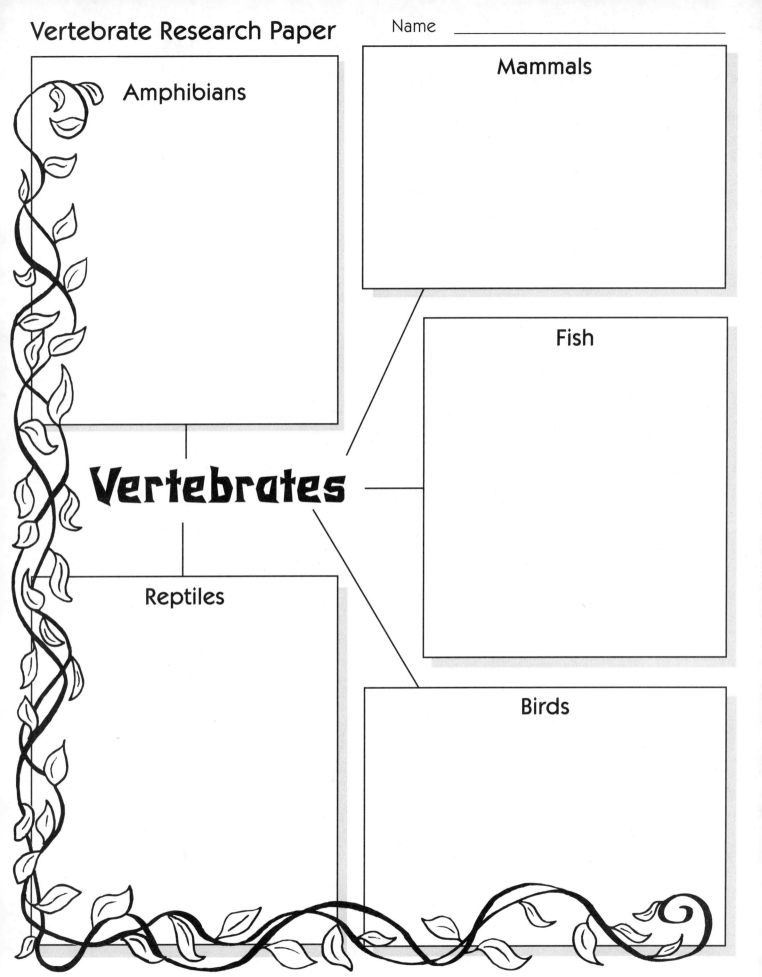

Amphibians

Mammals

Vertebrates

Fish

Reptiles

Birds

Use for introduction to vertebrates by defining these categories.

Name   <u>Risa Johanson</u>

Independently make your graphic organizer to reflect your research.

Sample

Birds lay eggs. Their eggs are in a hard shell.

Wings and feathers make birds different from other vertebrates.

Some birds have feathers but cannot fly.

Birds

All birds lose and replace their feathers during a year.

Nests can be made of twigs, leaves or feathers. They can also be made of mud or other substances birds find.

Foods birds eat include: nuts, seeds, oysters, fish, tiny water plants and animals.

Bones and feathers are made in a special way to help birds fly.

76

Name _____

Independently make your graphic organizer to reflect your research.

Independently make your graphic organizer to reflect your research.

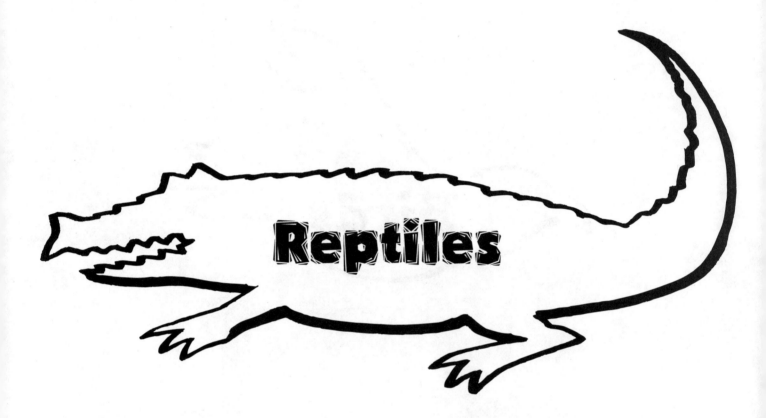

Independently make your graphic organizer to reflect your research.

Independently make your graphic organizer to reflect your research.

Independently make your graphic organizer to reflect your research.

Informational Paper Rubric

Sample

Student Name ___Risa Johanson___   Date ___10/11/98___

Format

Introductory Paragraph (definition of *vertebrates*, five groups identified)	5 pts.	5
Reptile Paragraph (definition and facts)	10 pts.	10
Bird Paragraph (definition and facts) *need more facts*	10 pts.	7
Amphibian Paragraph (definition and facts)	10 pts.	10
Fish Paragraph (definition and facts)	10 pts.	10
Mammal Paragraph (definition and facts)	10 pts.	10
Ending Paragraph (summary restating first paragraph)	5 pts.	5
Indentations	5 pts.	5
Capital Letters (beginning of sentences, proper nouns, abbreviations, etc.)	5 pts.	1
Sentence Endings (period, question mark, exclamation point)	5 pts.	4
Punctuation (commas, quotations, apostrophes, colons, etc.)	5 pts.	3
Context (omissions, additions, word usage, correct grammar) *was/were*	10 pts.	9
Spelling	10 pts.	8

vertebrates

oyster

Total 100 pts. 87% B

Comments: ___Super information and well written.___

Informational Paper Rubric

Student Name _____ Date _____

Format

    Introductory Paragraph (definition of *vertebrates*,
five groups identified)   5 pts. _____

    Reptile Paragraph (definition and facts)   10 pts. _____

    Bird Paragraph (definition and facts)   10 pts. _____

    Amphibian Paragraph (definition and facts)   10 pts. _____

    Fish Paragraph (definition and facts)   10 pts. _____

    Mammal Paragraph (definition and facts)   10 pts. _____

    Ending Paragraph (summary restating first paragraph)   5 pts. _____

Indentations   5 pts. _____

Capital Letters (beginning of sentences, proper nouns, abbreviations, etc.) 5 pts. _____

Sentence Endings (period, question mark, exclamation point)   5 pts. _____

Punctuation (commas, quotations, apostrophes, colons, etc.)   5 pts. _____

Context (omissions, additions, word usage, correct grammar)   10 pts. _____

Spelling   10 pts. _____

                                           Total 100 pts. _____

Comments: _____

_____

_____

Immigrant Diary

Day 1

Reason(s) for Leaving

_____

_____

_____

_____

Belongings Packed for the Trip

_____

_____

_____

_____

Days 2-4

Daily Life on the Ship

_____

_____

_____

_____

Dangers/Problems on the Ship

_____

_____

_____

_____

Day 5

Arrival in U.S.A. (examinations, money, language, etc.)

_____

_____

_____

_____

_____

Immigrant Diary Rubric

Student Name _____ Date _____

Format

    Day 1: Leaving homeland   20 pts. _____

    Days 2-4: Journey on the ship   30 pts. _____

    Day 5: Arrival in U.S.A.   10 pts. _____

Indentations   5 pts. _____

Capital Letters (beginning of sentences, proper nouns, abbreviations, etc.)   5 pts. _____

Sentence Endings (period, question mark, exclamation point)   5 pts. _____

Punctuation (commas, quotations, apostrophes, colons, etc.)   5 pts. _____

Context (omissions, additions, word usage, correct grammar)   10 pts. _____

Spelling   10 pts. _____

                                        Total   100 pts. _____

Comments: _____

_____

_____

CINQUAIN

A cinquain is a five-line poem.

Write a cinquain about yourself using the sample form below.

Line 1: Student's name

age, eye color, hair color, size

Line 2: Two adjectives or descriptive words

(I am a _____ person.)

Line 3: Three verbs that describe you (action)

Line 4: A simile (*like a* or *as a*)

Line 5: A synonym for the first line

Remember to write a rough draft first. Watch for your poem to be displayed.

CINQUAIN POEM

_____

_____

_____

_____

_____

Cinquain Rubric

Student Name _____   Date _____

Format

    Line 1: one word which states the subject   6 pts. _____

    Line 2: two words which describe the subject   14 pts. _____

    Line 3: three words which express action   14 pts. _____

    Line 4: a simile using *like a* or *as a*   14 pts. _____

    Line 5: one word which is a synonym for line 1   12 pts. _____

Indentations   5 pts. _____

Capital Letters (beginning of sentences, proper nouns, abbreviations, etc.)   5 pts. _____

Sentence Endings (period, question mark, exclamation point)   5 pts. _____

Punctuation (commas, quotations, apostrophes, colons, etc.)   5 pts. _____

Context (omissions, additions, word usage, correct grammar)   10 pts. _____

Spelling   10 pts. _____

Total   100 pts. _____

Comments: _____

_____

_____

Seven Poetry

_____
Name the group of seven.

_____
Tell what they are doing.

_____
_____
Describe the first in two lines.

_____
_____
_____
_____
_____
Describe the next five in one line each.

_____
_____
Describe the last in two lines concluding the poem.

Seven Poetry Example

Ball Players

There were seven ball players
Playing in the sun.
The first smacked the ball
And hit a home run.
The second grounded to first
The third tripled to third,
And the fourth was dying of thirst.
The fifth hit a double,
The sixth needed a Band-Aid™.
The seventh struck out quickly
And all drank Gatorade™.

TLC10111 Copyright © Teaching & Learning Company, Carthage, IL 62321-0010

Friendly Letter Rubric

Student Name _____ Date _____

Format: five parts included

    Heading   10 pts. _____

    Greeting   10 pts. _____

    Body   20 pts. _____

    Closing   10 pts. _____

    Signature   10 pts. _____

Indentations   5 pts. _____

Capital Letters (beginning of sentences, proper nouns, abbreviations, etc.)   5 pts. _____

Sentence Endings (period, question mark, exclamation point)   5 pts. _____

Punctuation (commas, quotations, apostrophes, colons, etc.)   5 pts. _____

Context (omissions, additions, word usage, correct grammar)   10 pts. _____

Spelling   10 pts. _____

                                                        Total   100 pts. _____

Comments: _____

_____

_____

Business Letter

_____ Heading
_____
_____

_____ Inside Address
_____
_____

_____ Greeting

Body
_____
_____
_____
_____
_____
_____
_____
_____
_____

_____ Closing
_____ Signature
_____ Print or type name

Business Letter Rubric

Student Name _____ Date _____

Format: six parts included

    Heading   10 pts. _____

    Inside Address   10 pts. _____

    Greeting   10 pts. _____

    Body   10 pts. _____

    Closing   10 pts. _____

    Signature   10 pts. _____

Indentations   5 pts. _____

Capital Letters (beginning of sentences, proper nouns, abbreviations, etc.)   5 pts. _____

Sentence Endings (period, question mark, exclamation point)   5 pts. _____

Punctuation (commas, quotations, apostrophes, colons, etc.)   5 pts. _____

Context (omissions, additions, word usage, correct grammar)   10 pts. _____

Spelling   10 pts. _____

                                             Total   100 pts. _____

Comments: _____

_____

_____

Chapter 4

Conclusion

When working with low-achieving or at-risk students, many considerations are needed. The ideas in this book have been used and developed in our classrooms over a long period of time. If the changes are made in your classroom one at a time, they will not be overwhelming or too time-consuming. Only you know what things will work for your students and what strategies would be most beneficial for you at this time.

The graphic organizers and rubrics can be used by anyone at any grade level. Depending on the grade level you teach, you may need to adapt or change the organizer or rubric. Use them with all your students, not just the low-achieving or at-risk ones.

We continually see new groups of students entering our classroom, afraid or unwilling to take a risk and learn something new. By the end of the year after using many of these strategies, we see bright, young students willing to take risks and finding success. You also will see results.